WHAT MAKES A MAN?

STUDY  GUIDE

Stephen Griffith and Bill Deckard

NAVPRESS
BRINGING TRUTH TO LIFE
NavPress Publishing Group
P.O. Box 35001, Colorado Springs, Colorado 80935

The Navigators is an international Christian organization. Jesus Christ gave His followers the Great Commission to go and make disciples (Matthew 28:19). The aim of The Navigators is to help fulfill that commission by multiplying laborers for Christ in every nation.

NavPress is the publishing ministry of The Navigators. NavPress publications are tools to help Christians grow. Although publications alone cannot make disciples or change lives, they can help believers learn biblical discipleship, and apply what they learn to their lives and ministries.

© 1993 by Still Point Press, Inc.
All rights reserved. No part of this publication may be reproduced in any form without written permission from NavPress, P.O. Box 35001, Colorado Springs, CO 80935.
ISBN 08910-97309

Some of the anecdotal illustrations in this book are true to life and are included with the permission of the persons involved. All other illustrations are composites of real situations, and any resemblance to people living or dead is coincidental.

Unless otherwise identified, all Scripture quotations in this publication are taken from the *HOLY BIBLE: NEW INTERNATIONAL VERSION®* (NIV®). Copyright © 1973, 1978, 1984 by International Bible Society. Used by permission of Zondervan Publishing House. All rights reserved. Other versions used include: the *New American Standard Bible* (NASB), © The Lockman Foundation 1960, 1962, 1963, 1968, 1971, 1972, 1973, 1975, 1977; and the *King James Version* (KJV).

Printed in the United States of America

5 6 7 8 9 10 11 12 13 14 15 / 99 98 97 96 95

Contents

What Are Promises?

People have been making and breaking promises since the dawn of human history. Since most promises made soon become promises broken, most people are somewhat philosophical about their skills as promise keepers. Among the assorted wisdom on the subject of promises we find the following:

> Promises and pie-crust are made to be broken.[1]

> Never promise more than you can perform. The man who promises everything is sure to fulfill nothing, and everyone who promises too much is in danger of using evil means in order to carry out his promises.[2]

DEFINING A PROMISE KEEPER

In their introductory chapter, Gary Smalley and John Trent go to the dictionary for a definition of the word *promise*: "What is a promise? Webster defines it as, 'to give a basis for hopes or expectations.' A promise giver is one who gives a basis for hopes and expectations and a promise keeper is one who fulfills those hopes and expectations" (page 16).

1. Do you agree or disagree with the dictionary definition? Explain.

2. a. What things have you personally said to people that have given them "a basis for hopes or expectations"?

   b. How well have you followed through on those promises?

3. In what ways do you hope to improve your "promise keeping skills" as a result of this series of studies?

4. What specific people in your life need the security or hope that a promise from you could give them?

5. Do you agree with the statement, "Keeping your promise holds its own reward" (page 16)? Explain.

6. What do the authors say are some of the rewards of promise keeping (page 16)?

Leighton Ford begins his section in chapter 1 with this statement: "Nothing binds us on to the other like a promise kept and nothing divides us like a promise broken" (page 17).

7. a. What blessings have you seen in your own life or in that of your family because of promises faithfully kept?

b. What negative consequences have you seen when you or someone close to you has failed to keep a promise?

Ford quotes Bill McCartney:

> We want to beat Notre Dame; and we want to be number one. But my real goal is to use what influence I have to help raise up a generation of promise keepers. I think we need people in our country who will be promise keepers—in our families, in our businesses, in our public life, in everything. (page 18)

8. a. To what extent do you agree with McCartney about the urgency of the need for promise keepers in our society today?

b. How do you see this need in each of the areas he lists?

• Family

● Business

● Public life

9. How well would you do on the "mirror test" Ford describes on pages 21-22?

GOD'S FAITHFULNESS AS A PROMISE KEEPER

Gary Oliver's dramatic story of his near-drowning ends with these thoughts: "When I made it to shore I was a bit embarrassed but most of all I was grateful. The lifeguard said he had been watching me. He could see there was a rip tide condition and knew I wasn't aware of it. Before I had gone under he was already swimming towards me to warn me and if necessary rescue me" (pages 26-27).

Oliver goes on to note that "God is our lifeguard." Here is one of the two passages from the psalms he mentions that describe God's care over us:

> I lift up my eyes to the hills—
>   where does my help come from?
> My help comes from the LORD,
>   the Maker of heaven and earth.
> He will not let your foot slip—
>   he who watches over you will not slumber;
> indeed, he who watches over Israel
>   will neither slumber nor sleep. (Psalm 121:1-4)

10. a. What has God promised to do (or *not* do!) on our behalf?

b. When has that truth been a comfort to you?

O LORD, you have searched me
    and you know me.
You know when I sit and when I rise;
    you perceive my thoughts from afar.
You discern my going out and my lying down;
    you are familiar with all my ways.
Before a word is on my tongue
    you know it completely, O LORD.
You hem me in—behind and before;
    you have laid your hand upon me. (Psalm 139:1-5)

11. What pictures come to your mind when the psalmist says that God "hems us in"?

These verses show how God faithfully fulfills His promises to His people:

"Praise be to the LORD, who has given rest to his people Israel just as he promised. Not one word has failed of all the good promises he gave through his servant Moses." (1 Kings 8:56)

No matter how many promises God has made, they are "Yes" in Christ. (2 Corinthians 1:20)

THE ROAD TEST
    1. Using a copy machine, make a "wanted" poster with your face on it! Below your photo, list all the people who "want" you to be a promise keeper for them, and list the "rewards" you will receive through your faithful promise keeping.

2. Take the "mirror test" as you leave for work the next few mornings. Can you look yourself in the eye, knowing that you are doing your best to be a man of integrity?

3. Using a study Bible or concordance, study God's promises and the way those promises were fulfilled.

PERSONAL CHECKLIST

1.

2.

3.

NOTES
1. Jonathan Swift, quoted in Robert Andrews, *The Concise Columbia Dictionary of Quotations* (New York: Columbia University Press, 1987), page 212.
2. Carl Jung, quoted in Andrews, page 212.

The Promises You Make to God

In the first lesson we studied about the importance of promises. We learned that God sets the example for us in being a promise keeper. Most importantly, He promised to raise Jesus from the dead, and on Easter morning, He kept that promise. As Christians, we stake our eternal destiny on the fact that God has kept that promise. In response, there are some promises we need to make to God. That will be our subject in this session. (In lessons 3-12 we will consider the promises we need to be making and keeping to various people in our lives.)

When God first called the nation of Israel to be His chosen people, He gave them a law to live by. We read in Exodus 24:7 that Moses "took the Book of the Covenant and read it to the people. They responded, 'We will do everything the LORD has said; we will obey.'"

1. What was Israel's promise to God?

History proved whether the Israelites were promise makers or promise keepers. These comments from the book of Hebrews give the sad conclusion:

"The time is coming, declares the Lord, when I will make a new covenant with the house of Israel and with the house of Judah. It will not be like the covenant I made with their forefathers when I took them by the hand to lead them out of Egypt, because they did not remain faithful to my covenant, and I turned away from them, declares the Lord." (Hebrews 8:8-9)

The requirements of God's law were fulfilled only by Jesus Christ, in His sinless life and in His death for our sins.

Going back to the passage we just looked at in Hebrews, let's get the "rest of the story":

"This is the covenant I will make with the house of Israel after that time, declares the Lord. I will put my laws in their minds and write them on their hearts. I will be their God, and they will be my people. No longer will a man teach his neighbor, or a man his brother, saying, 'Know the Lord,' because they will all know me, from the least of them to the greatest." (8:10-11)

2. a. Why did God choose to "make a new covenant with the house of Israel"?

   b. What promise does God make to us as a part of that new covenant?

   c. What promise should we make to Him?

d. What, according to these verses, gives us the power to keep that promise?

3. What do each of the verses that follow say about other promises we should make to God?

I have fought the good fight, I have finished the race, I have kept the faith. (2 Timothy 4:7)

Many of his disciples turned back and no longer followed him.

"You do not want to leave too, do you?" Jesus asked the Twelve.

Simon Peter answered him, "Lord, to whom shall we go? You have the words of eternal life." (John 6:66-68)

"If we are thrown into the blazing furnace, the God we serve is able to save us from it, and he will rescue us from your hand, O king. But even if he does not, we want you to know, O king, that we will not serve your gods or worship the image of gold you have set up." (Daniel 3:17-18)

"Be dressed ready for service and keep your lamps burning, like men waiting for their master to return from a wedding banquet, so that when he comes and knocks they can immediately open the door for him. It will be good for those servants whose master finds them watching when he comes." (Luke 12:35-37)

If you wonder about your ability to keep your promises to God, consider this wonderful passage at the close of Hebrews:

> May the God of peace, who through the blood of the eternal covenant brought back from the dead our Lord Jesus . . . equip you with everything good for doing his will, and may he work in us what is pleasing to him. (13:20-21)

4. Why is the Hebrew writer so confident that each and every one of us can be a faithful promise keeper?

Gary Smalley and John Trent point us to the advice found in Psalm 1 (page 29). It is good "resource material" for men who sincerely want to be promise keepers:

> Blessed is the man
> > who does not walk in the counsel of the wicked
> or stand in the way of sinners
> > or sit in the seat of mockers.
> But his delight is in the law of the LORD,
> > and on his law he meditates day and night.
> He is like a tree planted by streams of water,
> > which yields its fruit in season
> and whose leaf does not wither.
> > Whatever he does prospers. (Psalm 1:1-3)

5. a. In the situation where you live and work, is it easy or difficult to avoid "the counsel of the wicked"? Is it easy or difficult to avoid "standing in the way of sinners"?

b. Can you truly say, right now, that you "delight" in regular Bible study? Why is that?

c. How can gaining the things promised to you by God in these verses help you, in turn, to be a better promise keeper?

6. William Gaultiere says there are three wrong tracks men sometimes choose as we seek to become promise keepers (pages 30-31). On which, if any, of these have you at times found yourself?

❑ Guilt: making more and more promises, because you feel you'll never be the Christian man you want to be
❑ Pride: feeling like you have arrived, having finally succeeded in keeping all your promises
❑ Apathy: knowing you can't keep your promises, so you don't even try

7. a. Gaultiere reminds us of the parable of the prodigal son (Luke 15:11-32), which Jesus told to show us more about what God is really like. What, according to the parable, is God's attitude toward us when we fail to keep our promises?

b. How can this parable give us the right attitude toward keeping our promises to God and to the people in our lives?

Roger Palms talks about the need to find a fixed reference point for our lives:

> In a society without fixed points we have to decide to make our own or we will be adrift, and every action will have a counter thrust to it.
>
> Men have to be committed. Only those who determine that they will be, who have a reference point, will ever touch the world in a meaningful way. The Christian, with reference to the Rock and obedience to the high calling of God in Christ Jesus, has a reason for commitment. (page 33)

8. a. Do you agree that our society today has no fixed reference points? How do you see this demonstrated by the people you live and work with?

   b. How can the promises we make to God be the kind of reference points we need in life?

   c. What can we as Christian men do to help others find such a reference point for their lives?

Luis Palau tells the story of a little boy named Dominic who, when he got lost in the woods, survived by doing everything his father had told him to do in such a situation (pages 34-35). Palau draws a lesson for us from Dominic's example:

> Dominic reminds me of what we should do as men who are children of a loving and infinitely wise heavenly Father. We are not to walk according to the course of this world, which is passing away. Instead, we are to walk in obedience to the Lord's commands. After all, He knows what is best for us. That's one of the reasons I believe the Bible is so relevant for us today. (page 35)

9. Why is our obedience so important to our heavenly Father? (Why was Dominic's obedience so important to *his* father!)

The apostle Peter wrote about our attitude as we seek to obey God:

> As obedient children, do not conform to the evil desires you had when you lived in ignorance. But just as he who called you is holy, so be holy in all you do; for it is written: "Be holy, because I am holy." (1 Peter 1:14-16)

10. a. Why do you suppose Peter told us to be "obedient children," rather than "obedient adults"?

b. Why should we strive to be holy?

c. Should that be reason enough for us? Explain.

John Yates says that some men are "ladies' men" while others are "men's men" (pages 36-38). But as Christians, we should want to be "God's men."

11. According to the following description, how is "God's man" more than simply a "man's man"? Underline the phrases that stand out to you.

What does it mean to be God's man? It means being a man's man but more. To be God's man means to be the friend of God and the servant of God, who wants, above all, the will of God. God's man knows and trusts that God's way is the best way, and therefore commits himself daily to discerning, as best he can, the will of God in all situations. He sees his life, his abilities, his possessions, his family as gifts entrusted to him by God. All he has belongs to God. Living God's way matters more than anything else. (page 37)

Yates goes on to say that, "God's man is no carbon copy of another. He is an original who refuses to let others do his thinking for him" (page 38).

12. a. According to the following advice, how can each of us become "an original" as a Christian man?

Do not conform any longer to the pattern of this world, but be transformed by the renewing of your mind. (Romans 12:2)

b. How do you think a man goes about getting his mind renewed?

c. What steps do you need to take in your life right now to be "transformed" into God's man?

d. How can that transformation make you a better promise keeper, to God and to the important people in your life?

THE ROAD TEST

1. Borrowing the words of Psalm 1, set yourself a "day and night"—evening and morning—Bible reading schedule.

2. List the ways you have allowed other people to do your thinking for you. Alongside that list, make notes about how you will change each item to be more like how God would have you think and act.

3. Take notice of men you know who seem to be "God's men." Note ways that you can be more like them and work at putting those things into practice.

PERSONAL CHECKLIST

1.

2.

3.

The Promises You Make to Yourself

Chapters 3 through 5 of *What Makes a Man?* deal respectively with the promises you make to yourself, to your wife, and to your family.

Gary Smalley and John Trent set the stage for these three chapters by highlighting five qualities a Christian man should have (pages 39-47):

- Assertiveness
- Self-control
- Independence
- Self-confidence
- Stability

Here's how they introduce these five character qualities: "If you could somehow freeze-frame biblical manhood or in some way boil it down into its component parts, you would see five elements that are always present. These key ingredients can be learned by a woman, but they set a man apart as a man. All of them are powerful reflections of the kind of man Jesus Christ was, and of what we need to be as well" (page 39).

They divide the five qualities in this way:

Promises to yourself
    Assertiveness
    Self-control

Promises to your wife
   Independence
   Self-confidence

Promises to your family
   Stability

Smalley and Trent point out that these character qualities apply in many different situations, but are especially
good to incorporate into our relationships with our wives and
families, and our inner lives as individual men. As we look
at chapters 3 through 5, we'll keep coming back to these five
characteristics.

ASSERTIVENESS
Smalley and Trent introduce the character quality of assertiveness by pointing to our Lord Himself:

> When you look at the person of Christ, you're looking
> at assertiveness. He healed the lame on the Sabbath
> day, even when the religious leaders stood in His face
> and dared Him to do so. He cast money-changers
> from the temple and tossed verbal bombshells at the
> Pharisees. . . . He chased away demons and faced
> up to the prince of darkness. In all these situations
> He relied on the healthy assertion of His power.
> (pages 39-40)

1. Does this picture of Jesus match the way you usually
   think of Him? Do you think that is the way most people
   think of Him? (How do most people see Him?)

The authors go on to talk about the "natural assertiveness" of
men. They give an example of how little boys tend to be more
aggressive than little girls. Then the authors claim, "It is our

deepest nature as men to push forward, to step out, to take charge, to fight for the higher ground" (page 40).

2. What events in your life do those phrases bring to mind? (Do you see yourself as being too assertive or not assertive enough? Explain.)

3. a. When in your life, if ever, have you been as unassertive as the "passive man" the authors describe (page 41)?

   b. Think about the "angry all the time" personality they describe in the next section. When have you ever fit that description?

Notice how the authors describe Jesus as an example of assertiveness: "Jesus' inner assertiveness didn't make Him less attractive as a man; it added to His ability to lead others. But His strength was always tempered in love, not testing or tyrannical" (page 42).
Consider these two pictures of Jesus:

Jesus entered the temple area and drove out all who were buying and selling there. He overturned the table of the money changers and the benches of those selling doves. "It is written," he said to them, "'My house will be called a house of prayer,' but you are making it a 'den of robbers.'" (Matthew 21:12-13)

27

He was oppressed and afflicted,
    yet he did not open his mouth;
he was led like a lamb to the slaughter,
    and as a sheep before her shearers is silent,
    so he did not open his mouth. (Isaiah 53:7)

4. Isaiah was prophesying about Jesus' willing submission to death on the cross. Can you believe that these words describe the same Person who drove out the money-changers? How do you explain these differing aspects of Christ's personality?

5. a. Think about various situations you'll be facing in the next few days. In which of those situations will you need to be especially assertive?

   b. In which might you need to remain silent?

SELF-CONTROL

The authors give vivid examples of what self-control is all about:

Self-control is the strength to keep your tongue still when everyone else at work is ripping the boss to shreds behind his back. It's the resolve to turn past the

28

"late night" movie selection in the hotel room, even when you're all alone. It's the courage to count to ten, and then to ten again, instead of ripping into your spouse or teenager when she irritates you. (page 44)

6. Thinking back to recent events in your life, what examples of self-control (or lack thereof) could you cite?

Proverbs 15:32 states, "He who ignores discipline despises himself." Smalley and Trent say, "The degree of self-control you have in your life is in direct proportion to the degree of acceptance you have for yourself" (page 44).

7. Do you suppose ignoring discipline shows that you despise yourself? Explain.

8. In what areas of life do you struggle most with self-control? (Money? Food? Certain sexual issues? Work? Anger at family?)

Read carefully Larry Crabb's description of a "manly man" (pages 48-49). Crabb says that such a man is "ambitious for God's glory" and is concerned about the needs of others more than he is about his own needs. He goes on to say that this "manly" man "feels a completion and wholeness that make selfish achievement and immoral pleasures less appealing."

9. How could a greater focus on God and on the needs of others help you overcome temptations like worldly success and sexual immorality?

10. How is the manly man Crabb describes different from the male role models thrown at us by Hollywood?

11. a. Be totally honest. Which model of the "real man" do you find more appealing—Hollywood's model or the one Crabb presents? Why?

    b. Which of these two kinds of men do you suspect will find more lasting satisfaction in life? Explain.

12. What makes striving to become a godly man a promise worth making to yourself?

13. Ken Abraham talks about men who are successful in various pursuits but still feel like "losers" in terms of their spiritual life (pages 56-57). Can you identify with that feeling?

14. a. How can these verses help you find greater success in your walk with the Lord?

"Not by might nor by power, but by my Spirit," says the LORD of hosts. (Zechariah 4:6, NASB)

Christ in you, the hope of glory. (Colossians 1:27)

b. In your own words, what's the key to achieving real self-control and a strong spiritual life?

c. Why is the advice given in these verses so hard for most men to accept?

Steve Farrar describes two extremes we can go to in our spiritual lives (pages 58-59). He calls these "spiritual anorexia" and "spiritual bulimia." Spiritual anorexia means starving ourselves of the nourishment we need from God's Word.

15. Are you starving yourself of God's Word? If so, what are some of the things you try to feed on instead?

Some of us study the Bible too little. But do others study it too much? This passage from the book of James sheds light on the cause and cure of spiritual bulimia:

> Anyone who listens to the word but does not do what it says is like a man who looks at his face in a mirror and, after looking at himself, goes away and immediately forgets what he looks like. But the man who looks intently into the perfect law that gives freedom, and continues to do this, not forgetting what he has heard, but doing it—he will be blessed in what he does. (James 1:23-25)

16. a. What's the cause of spiritual bulimia?

    b. Can we cure spiritual bulimia by "cutting back" on Bible study? How do we cure it?

Bill Hybels reminds us that "burnout" can come from a lack of diet, sleep, or exercise (page 60).

17. a. How are you doing in these three areas?

    • Diet

- Sleep

- Exercise

b. What steps can you take in the next few days to begin doing better in each area?

- Diet

- Sleep

- Exercise

c. Do you see these steps as "promises to yourself"? Are they promises worth keeping? Explain.

THE ROAD TEST

1. Read several Bible passages about the life of Jesus. After each passage, pause and think about how He exemplified assertiveness and self-control in that passage.

2. Write down the names of male movie stars or other "celebrities" you admire. Beside their names note the character traits they exhibit and whether you, as a Christian, should or should not try to imitate that trait.

3. Following the advice of James 1:23–25, jot down at least one solid practical application each time you read the Bible. Make it something you think you will actually do—a promise you intend to keep!

PERSONAL CHECKLIST

1.

2.

3.

The Promises You Make
to Your Wife

If you're single, you may feel that this lesson doesn't apply to you. But read it—you may not be single forever!

Now we come to the promises we make to a person who would not even be a part of our life except for a promise we once made to her. Was that initial promise enough to build a lasting marriage, or must we go on making—and keeping—promises to that most important person in our life? Gary Smalley and John Trent say that two character qualities especially needed for a strong marriage are *independence* and *self-confidence* (pages 61-68). In this lesson we'll be looking at what they mean by independence and why self-confidence is so necessary to a good marriage.

INDEPENDENCE
1. The authors explain independence by giving an example of its opposite—co-dependence. Have you known men like "good old Russ" (page 62), who seem to have no ability to stand up for themselves? What do you see as the common traits they exhibited?

The authors ask some sobering questions to help us each assess our level of independence as men:

Can you make decisions without looking over your shoulder at Mom and Dad (not for counsel, but for permission)? Are you able to say, "I don't like that" to another person, without unreasonable fear that they'll say, "I don't like you"? And even if something you stand for isn't popular, do you have the inner strength to stand apart from the crowd and lean only on the rightness of your action? (page 63)

2. Why is a "yes" answer to each of these questions important to a good marriage?

3. How do you as a man achieve the proper balance between "honoring" your father and mother and "leaving" them (Ephesians 5:31, 6:2)?

A husband who exhibits a healthy independence is essential to a marriage:

If you seek to achieve that healthy independence, your wife will be able to know and respect the true you. She will see the real personality, the real decision-maker you can be. It will be the most important step you ever make toward a healthy interdependence with her. (page 64)

4. How would a good sense of independence on your part lead to a "healthy interdependence" between you and your wife? Give an example related to a decision you are making or have made.

SELF-CONFIDENCE

Another necessary factor for a good marriage, say Smalley and Trent, is *self-confidence*:

> Self-confidence is what everyone else in the locker room looks like they have before you hit the field for the big game, or get ready to hit your ball off the first tee. Actually, self-confidence is more than that look of determination, that purposeful step, the firmness in a handshake. It's that inner security of knowing who you are . . . and where you'll spend eternity. (page 64)

The authors suggest two key ingredients that will help us have the firm handshake of self-confidence: *credibility* and *credentials*. Credibility simply means telling the truth. Self-confidence will come as we know with certainty that we have nothing to hide.

Abraham Lincoln said, "I always tell the truth. . . . That way I only have to remember half as much" (page 65).

If we're hiding something, we're standing on thin ice. There's always the chance that someday, in some unexpected way, you'll pick up the phone and the secret will come out.

5. a. Have you experienced the fear that a dark secret from your past will come out? How has that affected your relationship with your wife and family?

   b. Have you experienced the "boldness" that comes from a clear conscience? How has that boldness helped you be a better husband and father?

The other key component of self-confidence is *credentials*. As Smalley and Trent explain,

> If the first building block of self-confidence is credibility, the second is just as important—credentials. Not necessarily the kind that put letters behind your name, but the kind that put a track record of excellence behind your efforts.
>
> There is nothing that builds self-confidence quicker than excellence. Whether it's hitting the grade line right on the mark in your D-9 PushCat, getting a client's tax return to them early, or lining up seams on the wallpaper so they seem to disappear . . . excellence breeds confidence. (page 65)

6. a. Recall times when you have experienced the confidence that comes from a job well done. What were the key ingredients to arriving at that place of satisfaction and accomplishment?

   b. What challenges in your life right now call for the application of those same ingredients?

7. The authors tell two very different stories—one about a job well done, and one about shoddy workmanship. What kind of attitudes cause some people to be satisfied with second best in their work?

Our own self-confidence can give our wives a greater sense of self-confidence:

If healthy independence builds healthy interdependence, then a husband's self-confidence surely gives
his wife a deeper sense of security. A healthy self-
confidence will in turn transfer over to your wife and
help her feel a similar self-confidence. In turn, it also
gives her the security to allow her husband to lead the
family. (page 68)

Consider this instruction: "Wives, submit to your husbands as
to the Lord. For the husband is the head of the wife as Christ
is the head of the church, his body, of which he is the Savior"
(Ephesians 5:22-23).

8. a. Why do you think wives are instructed to submit to
their husbands?

  b. How does a man's self-confidence help his wife
  do this?

  c. Should a Christian husband ever *demand* that his wife
  submit to him? Explain.

9. The verse before the instruction to wives says, "Submit
to one another out of reverence for Christ" (Ephesians
5:21). Does this mean that husbands, in some situations,
should submit to their wives? Why do you say that?

A parallel passage in Colossians says, "Husbands, love your wives, and be not bitter against them" (3:19, KJV). Ken Taylor tells how that truth was made real in his own life (pages 69-71).

10. a. Do you harbor bitterness against your wife? For what?

   b. Is forgiveness something you can "promise" your wife? Why, or why not?

Read about how submitting to each other helped Dennis Rainey and his wife deal with a marital conflict quickly (pages 78-79).

   John Yates relates that, on his wedding day, he made a promise that he would pray with his wife at least once a day (pages 72-73). He lists four reasons why he feels that promise has helped strengthen his marriage.

11. Explain each of those four reasons in your own words.

12. Have you had a similar experience with prayer in your own marriage? If so, describe how prayer has helped. If not, why do you suppose you haven't prayed with your wife? What makes it hard for you to do that?

13. Donald Harvey talks about taking responsibility for the mistakes we make in our marriages (pages 74-75). Do you agree that "Real men accept responsibility for their behavior"? Based on that definition, how many "real men" do you know?!

14. a. As Harvey observes, the "blame game" goes all the way back to Adam and Eve. Why is it so easy to blame others for our mistakes?

    b. Why can it be damaging to a marriage to do so?

Ken Brown (pages 76-77) found that two very different women wanted similar things from men:

- A man who was honest and could earn their confidence and trust.
- A man who was sensitive and caring, truly interested in their needs.
- A man who was loyal, always willing to protect them from those who didn't have their best interests at heart.
- A man who was faithful, never betraying the bond between them.
- A man whose love was freely given and unconditional, letting the woman enjoy acceptance.
- A man who cherished the woman, acknowledging her value and importance to him.

Compare this list to the description of Christian love below. How many of the six items desired by modern women are on the 2000-year-old list?

> Love is patient, love is kind. It does not envy, it does not boast, it is not proud. It is not rude, it is not self-seeking, it is not easily angered, it keeps no record of wrongs. Love does not delight in evil but rejoices with the truth. It always protects, always trusts, always hopes, always perseveres. (1 Corinthians 13:4-7)

15. a. According to Ephesians 5:28-29, why should a husband love his wife like that?

    b. What does it mean to love your wife "as your own body"?

    c. Explain the statement, "He who loves his wife loves himself." Is it equally true that "he who hates his wife hates himself"?

16. Look back at Ken Brown's list of six qualities. Put a star next to those you think you need to work on.

> The image of Christ is the standard God imprints on the soul of every woman. She may consciously decide to lower this standard and accept less, but it will not be what she wants. Less than the standard will not make her happy. Less than the standard will not fulfill her. (page 77)

17. How do you feel about being expected to measure up to "the standard God imprints on the soul of every woman"?

All Scripture is God-breathed and is useful for teaching, rebuking, correcting and training in righteousness, so that the man of God may be thoroughly equipped for every good work. (2 Timothy 3:16-17)

Being confident of this, that he who began a good work in you will carry it on to completion until the day of Christ Jesus. (Philippians 1:6)

If we confess our sins, he is faithful and just and will forgive us our sins and purify us from all unrighteousness. (1 John 1:9)

If any of you lacks wisdom, he should ask God, who gives generously to all without finding fault, and it will be given to him. (James 1:5)

In the same way, the Spirit helps us in our weakness. We do not know what we ought to pray for, but the Spirit himself intercedes for us with groans that words cannot express. (Romans 8:26)

18. God can truly help us if we sincerely seek His ideal standard for our lives as husbands. How can we, as Christian men, help each other measure up?

Charles Stanley shares some thoughts about romantic love:

> A woman would like to live her whole life experiencing romantic love because God made women to be loved. If you have lost all traces of your romantic days of courtship, you are a big loser. Sex, love, and romance are not always synonymous but they can be, and they are for the complete man.
>
> Romantic love reaches out in little way, showing attention and admiration. Romantic love remembers what pleases a woman, what excites her and what surprises her. Its action whispers: You are the most special person in my life. (page 82)

You may be surprised to find that romantic love with a wife rates a whole book in the Bible. Read Song of Songs 4:9-10—

> You have stolen my heart, my sister, my bride;
>   you have stolen my heart
> with one glance of your eyes,
>   with one jewel of your necklace.
> How delightful is your love, my sister, my bride!
>   How much more pleasing is your love than wine,
>   and the fragrance of your perfume than any spice!

19. a. Did you ever feel like that toward your wife? Do you now? If not, why not?

    b. What can you do to cultivate such an attitude toward her?

"Real men don't . . ." says Steve Farrar (pages 80-81), and we learn very quickly the rest of that thought: Real men don't commit adultery. Farrar presents Roger Staubach as exhibit A:

I remember a number of years ago watching Phyllis George interview Dallas Cowboy superstar Roger Staubach. It was a typical, dull sort of interview until Phyllis blindsided the quarterback with this question: "Roger, how do you feel when you compare yourself with Joe Namath, who is so sexually active and has a different woman on his arm every time we see him?"

We've all seen Staubach keep his cool in pressure game situations, and the tension in the air this time was just as great. But once again, Staubach kept his cool.

"Phyllis," he said calmly, "I'm sure I'm just as sexually active as Joe. The difference is that all of mine is with one woman."

Touchdown! Roger hit the end zone with that comeback. Real men don't commit adultery. A real man sticks with one woman. Period. (page 80)

20. How do you think Staubach was able to manage sexually active faithfulness? (Was he a super saint? Was his wife exceptionally sexy?)

21. What attitudes and conditions in your life do you need to keep you content with being faithful?

THE ROAD TEST

1. What decisions have you been putting off, at work or at home? Set a "deadline" for making that decision; bring it to God in prayer; seek the counsel of two or three trusted Christian friends; then . . . make the decision!

2. Are you lacking self-confidence because of a tendency to do less than your best? Think of some task you have performed in a less-than-satisfactory manner, and if possible, go back and do it right. If that is not possible, commit yourself to do your best on a task currently at hand.

3. Are there things your wife is interested in doing that you don't particularly care for? Surprise her by taking her to that concert, or going on a "garage sale marathon" together. (You just might enjoy it!)

PERSONAL CHECKLIST

1.

2.

3.

The Promises You Make
to Your Family

*Even if you don't currently have children, read through the following
lesson to start your thinking toward developing the vital trait of stability.*

Having dealt with the most important human relationship in
a married man's life—the husband-wife relationship—we come
to one that is surely a close second: the promises we make, as a
father, to our family.

Does your family more closely resemble the Waltons or
the Simpsons? Gary Smalley and John Trent (pages 83-86)
introduce the topic of our family responsibilities by discussing
the fifth trait of Christian manhood: *stability*—surely a trait
exemplified more by Mr. Walton than by the father in that
recent TV household.

STABILITY
The authors open with this claim: "Stability, it turns out, is
perhaps the number-one hope of a wife for her family life"
(page 83).

1. From your observations of your own wife and other
   women, would you agree with this assessment? Explain.

2. Have you seen homes where stability was notoriously lacking? Have you, on the other hand, seen homes that were examples of the blessings of stability? What role did the father play in increasing or decreasing stability?

The authors tell the incredible story of Second Lt. Bobo, whose almost super-human example of stability during combat in Vietnam led to his own death while saving the lives of many of his men.

3. a. Have you personally known men who have sacrificed for others in heroic ways? Who?

   b. Have you ever had to sacrifice your own desires to provide the stability your family needed? Describe what you did.

Consider these thoughts Smalley and Trent share from their experience in counseling:

> We are absolutely sick of talking of men who have "lost their feelings" for their spouse and decided it's simply easier to get a new one. Of course it is! At least in the short run. But soon that newfound person who is so "easy" to love will pile on just as many demands . . . until it's time for family number three . . . or four.

If we are truly men, then we'll dig in when the times get tough. We'll stay with the pain and be "trained" by it, rather than relying on our "feelings" and breaking our promises—at least if we're serious about being like Christ. (page 86)

4. How can being "serious about being like Christ" help us demonstrate manly stability no matter what our situation?

John Brown talks about the need to show fatherly love to our children—especially to our daughters (pages 87-89). Noting how a teenage daughter's "budding womanhood" can cause a father to begin withholding physical expressions of fatherly love, he quotes this observation from Jim Conway of Talbot Theological Seminary:

Studies show that girls who have a lot of appropriate, affectionate touch from their parents, and especially from their fathers, do not usually get married as young as those whose fathers ignore them. . . . Appropriate affection meets their need for physical closeness and causes them to take time to make a serious marriage choice. (page 88)

5. An aspect of "promising" our daughters a healthy marriage is purposing in our hearts to show them proper fatherly affection. What other emotional benefits can we promise our children as they grow into adulthood?

Steve Brown shares very personal thoughts about being the "father of the bride" (pages 90-94). He talks about such things as God's faithfulness in his family's life and the uncertainty of the future as he watches his daughters leave home—knowing they face great challenges but also knowing they have had a solid foundation in their home life.

6. Take a moment and jot down some thoughts you have had during various times of major transition in your children's lives. (What were your feelings at the time of those events? Have those feelings changed as you now look back?)

Just about everyone reading this study guide can probably relate to Don Osgood's section on family finances (pages 95-97). He observes,

> Where most of us are concerned, economic stress boils down to family finances. The problem is that we let our family finances get out of hand. First thing we know we're on a treadmill. It's no longer a case of joy from beating the system. The system has the upper hand. The little snowball at the top of the hill has become a smothering giant as it rolls down the hill toward us. That's the stressful predicament we get into with family finances. But there is a way out. (page 96)

7. Osgood notes that there are actually two ways out: Getting our spending under control, and dealing with the *spiritual causes* of our financial predicament. If you are

currently having financial difficulty in your home, how could any of these spiritual problems be to blame?

- Greed

- Self-love

- Lack of priorities

"So do not worry, saying, 'What shall we eat?' or 'What shall we drink?' or 'What shall we wear?' For the pagans run after all these things, and your heavenly Father knows that you need them. But seek first his kingdom and his righteousness, and all these things will be given to you as well." (Matthew 6:31-33)

8. How is this passage relevant to your financial problems?

Some thoughts from the apostle Paul suggest how our attitude toward material things can affect family life: "Godliness with contentment is great gain. For we brought nothing into the world, and we can take nothing out of it. But if we have food and clothing, we will be content with that" (1 Timothy 6:6-8).

9. What kind of home life could result from the "contentment" described in these verses?

10. How can you promise your family financial stability, without falling into the trap of materialism and all the problems it can bring to a family?

Ken Canfield reemphasizes the need for us to be stable and consistent as fathers, pointing to the Lord Himself as our example (pages 98-99). God is the "Father of the heavenly lights, who does not change like shifting shadows" (James 1:17).

11. a. Canfield talks about fathers being a "reference point" to help their children come to know the heavenly Father. How can we be a reference point to our children in the following areas?

- Our moral standards

- Our priorities in life

- The way we discipline them

- The love we show their mother and them

b. In which of these areas are you doing the best? In which would you like to see some improvement?

Do you ever worry about what your children could be learning at school? Fran Sciacca says we should also be thinking about what our children are learning at home—from us! He calls this the "informal curriculum" (pages 104-105). Even though the home is not like a formal classroom, important lessons are learned there—for good or for ill.

12. Sciacca tells about a time when he "taught" his children by a wrong example he set. What are you teaching your children by each of the following?

   ● The way you drive

   ● Your attitude toward your job

   ● Your personal devotional life

   ● The way you treat their mother

   ● Your general attitude toward life

   ● Your attitude about church attendance

   ● Your choice of TV viewing or other entertainment

Jay Carty tells how his father gave up a lucrative "career" in gambling in order to regain his son's respect (pages 100-101). Jerry Jenkins relates an incident where a parent's example taught a child dishonesty (pages 102-103).

13. Choose one item from question 12 that you think you need to change.

You would probably never think of leaving your younger children "home alone." But how much of the time are they home without their father? Chuck Miller tells very honestly how he was brought face to face with his own failure to spend enough time with his son (pages 106-107). And he asks some soul-searching questions:

> How are your children doing? Do they have hobbies and interests? Are you an active participant with them in their hobbies and interests? What's happening between you and each child in your family? Is there laughter? Do you invite them to pray for you about things in your life? Do they invite you to pray for things in their lives? Are you raising your children as human doers, or are you making time for them to become human beings? What might you be to each of your children this week? Pray God will give you hints and the power to do it. (page 107)

14. a. How do you react to those questions?

   b. Underline one that seems especially relevant, and explain why you chose that one.

If ever there was a child who needed stability, it is the child of divorced parents. Ken Canfield touches on this subject briefly (page 108). If you are divorced, ask your pastor or a knowledgeable Christian friend to help you meet the tremendous challenge you face as a father.

THE ROAD TEST

1. Set a regular weekly time to do something with each of your children.

2. Carefully observe your children to see if they have picked up any of your bad habits. Admit to them your failing in that area, and suggest that you and they could work together at conquering that particular habit.

3. Have a "Dark Ages Week," where you leave the television off for an entire week. See how many creative things your family can find to fill the time you would have spent watching television.

PERSONAL CHECKLIST

1.

2.

3.

The Promises You Make to Your Parents

Few of us grow to adulthood without a certain number of resentful feelings toward our parents. The process of becoming parents ourselves can give us a new perspective, as we see ourselves making some of the same mistakes our parents made.

One well-known nonChristian thinker, Oscar Wilde, says that few people are able to forgive their parents for the mistakes they supposedly made:

> Children begin by loving their parents. After a time they judge them. Rarely, if ever, do they forgive them.[1]

1. What is your opinion of Oscar Wilde's generalization? (Do you agree, or do you think he is being too pessimistic?)

Compare these words from the prophet Micah with Wilde's sober assessment of parent-child relations:

> Do not trust a neighbor;
>> put no confidence in a friend.
> Even with her who lies in your embrace
>> be careful of your words.
> For a son dishonors his father,

a daughter rises up against her mother . . .
a man's enemies are the members of his own
household. (Micah 7:5-6)

American humorist Mark Twain had a somewhat different perspective on how adult children view their parents:

When I was a boy of fourteen, my father was so igno-
rant I could hardly stand to have the old man around.
But when I got to be twenty-one, I was astonished at
how much he had learned in seven years.[2]

2. Do you think Wilde or Twain is more accurate in his
   view of parent-child relationships? Why?

Whatever our feelings are toward our parents, as they grow older we need to "promise" them that we will move beyond those feelings and be there when they need us. Harold Bussell talks about the importance of honoring our parents even though they may have failed us in various ways (pages 110-111). God commanded us, "Honor your father and your mother, so that you may live long in the land the LORD your God is giving you" (Genesis 20:12).

3. What conditions must our parents meet in order to
   deserve our honor?

4. What do you think it means to honor a parent who
   is cruel?

5. What do you think it would look like for you to honor your parents personally and financially?

6. a. The apostle Paul said that the command about honoring our fathers and mothers is "the first commandment with promise" (Ephesians 6:2). What is the promise?

   b. What do you think about that?

7. Would you want your children to treat you the way you treat your own parents? (How about the way you *talk about* your parents?) Explain.

Bussell urges us to adopt a positive view of old age:

> Old age does not have to mean infirmity of the character and soul of your parents. The Bible presents the mountain peak of life as old age. Why? Because character does not happen by attending a retreat or

memorizing Bible verses. Character is the byproduct
of a lifelong process. The elderly do have something
to teach us. The elderly are untapped wells of insight,
wisdom, and ministry. (page 111)

Consider these biblical exhortations about the dignity of older
people and of our parents in particular: "Rise in the presence
of the aged, show respect for the elderly and revere your
God" (Leviticus 19:32); and "Listen to your father, who gave
you life, and do not despise your mother when she is old"
(Proverbs 23:22).

8. If the Bible presents such a positive view of old age, why
   do you think many primitive, nonChristian societies treat
   their old people with more respect than we do in "Christian" America?

9. How do you think showing respect for the elderly relates
   to the decision about whether to put a parent in a nursing
   home?

10. Bussell tells about giving his elderly grandmother the
    opportunity to participate in his ministry through prayer
    (page 111). How can you help your parents and grand-
    parents feel that they still have a significant place in life?

11. Dave Simmons tells about how he found himself making the same mistakes with his son that his own father had made with him (pages 114-121). How might the following statement from the Old Testament relate to Simmons' experience of repeating his father's mistakes?

"He [God] punishes the children and their children for the sin of the fathers to the third and fourth generation." (Exodus 34:7)

That biblical truth has been demonstrated time and again throughout history, as children turn out "just like their parents." However, according to Jeremiah's prophecy of God's new covenant in Christ, we as Christians do not have to feel bound by the curse of generational sin:

"In those days people will no longer say,
    'The fathers have eaten sour grapes,
        and the children's teeth are set on edge.'
Instead, everyone will die for his own sin; whoever eats sour grapes—his own teeth will be set on edge." (Jeremiah 31:29-30)

12. a. What has been your own experience with "generational sin"?

b. Have you experienced the power of Christ to free you from that curse? Explain.

61

13. a. Considering Simmons' effort at "sonning" (being a good son), how can this help break the generational cycle of sin (page 117)?

b. Are there ways in which you can help your parents break bad habits passed down to them by their own parents? Name some possibilities.

14. Though he doesn't go into detail, Simmons says he used "secret love techniques" to improve his relationship with his father. What "secret" techniques might benefit your situation?

THE ROAD TEST
   1. See how many "childhood stories" you can draw out of your parents. One way to facilitate this would be to sit down with them and look through an old photo album.
   2. Make a list of areas of your life where you could benefit from your parents' advice, and make it a point to work these into conversations with them.
   3. For Father's Day or Mother's Day, help your children

stage a "This Is Your Life" for Grandpa or Grandma. This could include surprise appearances by their long-time friends who live nearby or humorous reenactments of episodes from their lives.

PERSONAL CHECKLIST
  1.

  2.

  3.

NOTES
  1. Oscar Wilde, quoted in Robert Andrews, *The Concise Columbia Dictionary of Quotations* (New York: Columbia University Press, 1987), page 188.
  2. Mark Twain, quoted in Andrews, page 95.

The Promises You Make to Your Friends

As Christians we strive to attain ideals like "loving our enemies." In reality, we could benefit from worldly advice like that of American journalist E. W. Howe: "Instead of loving your enemies, treat your friends a little better."[1]

The Bible has much to say about how we should treat our friends. It talks about the value of friendships. But according to the authors of chapter 7, for most men in present-day America the first issue to address is simply how to have any friends at all.

In their introduction to this chapter, Gary Smalley and John Trent give an example of true friendship, then state, "We men dream of friendships like that, but we seldom have them" (page 125).

1. a. If you agree, how would you explain this "epidemic of friendlessness" among men? If you disagree, why do you think people have this perception?

b. Do you tend to feel that most other men have more friends than you have? What gives you this impression?

If Smalley and Trent are right, perhaps you aren't really doing any worse than other men in the friendship department. Robert Hicks agrees (pages 136-137). He says that, while men often admire the kind of "good ole boy" friendships portrayed in beer commercials, few ever experience such friendships in real life:

> For men, even our friendships do not come easy. They are complicated, rarely evaluated, and never talked about. In the final analysis, once we marry and have kids, if friendships don't happen with the people we work with, they probably will never happen at all. . . .
> Many men place no priority on forming male-to-male relationships. There is no way I can convince these men that friendship is important. (pages 136-137)

2. If you do not presently have many close friends, why is that? (Is it by your own choice, or would you sincerely like to have more friends?)

3. Have certain experiences caused you to "shy away from" friendships with other men? (If you have experienced the kind of betrayal by friends described by Edwin Louis Cole [pages 138-139], have you decided not to pursue

friends? Or, do you think close friendships would be good, if only you could learn how to go about it?) Talk a little about this.

Tim Kimmel reports having wondered if he had six friends who would willingly drop everything to be pallbearers at his funeral (pages 134-135).

4. Who are your six closest friends? Are you consciously seeking to build and maintain those relationships?

Smalley and Trent end their introduction with a challenge: "As you read more about friendship in this section, ask yourself, 'Am I only looking for friends, or am I seeking to *be* a friend?'" (page 125).

5. What are some ways you could take the initiative to be a friend to a specific person you know?

The Bible says this about the true friend: "A friend loves at all times, and a brother is born for adversity" (Proverbs 17:17).

6. a. What are the characteristics of true friendship?

b. How can the pressures of family, church, and work responsibilities prevent such friendship from happening?

7. a. A popular song talked about how some people "love things and use people."[2] How can the pressure of the work-a-day world tempt us to "use" even our friends?

b. How can that prevent true friendship from developing?

Anyone who has been to Christian weddings is familiar with the statement, "It is not good for man to be alone" (Genesis 2:18). Jerry Bridges suggests that this applies to friendship as much as to marriage (pages 126-127).

8. a. Thinking in terms of friendship, what are the dangers of isolating ourselves from other people?

b. What positive results have you seen in your own life or in the lives of others when time is made for friendship?

Bridges goes on to state that "None of us has the spiritual wherewithal to 'go it alone' in the Christian life" (page 127).

9. The truth of that statement seems obvious enough—so why do you think many of us *try* to "go it alone" as Christians?

Bridges points to an interesting verse in Proverbs, which suggests one very good reason for friendship between Christian men: "As iron sharpens iron, so one man sharpens another" (27:17).

10. In what ways could you "sharpen" the faith and character of those in your circle of friends?

11. Have you ever experienced the kind of friendship described by Bob Belz (page 140)? Have you ever been that kind of friend to someone else? How did they respond?

A man of many companions may come to ruin, but there is a friend who sticks closer than a brother. (Proverbs 18:24)

12. a. In what ways can "many companions" be a bad thing?

b. Are "beer commercial friendships" more like what the verse describes as "many companions" or like a close friendship?

Chuck Miller tells briefly about the benefits of meeting with a group of Christian men on a regular basis—once every two weeks, in his case (pages 130-131).

13. What does or doesn't appeal to you about being a part of a "spiritual support group"?

Miller says of his group, "They give me insight, they correct me, they bother me" (page 131). "Correcting" and "bothering" may not sound like exactly what we want from friends.

> Wounds from a friend can be trusted, but an enemy multiplies kisses. (Proverbs 27:6)

> Encourage one another daily, as long as it is called Today, so that none of you may be hardened by sin's deceitfulness. (Hebrews 3:13)

> Let us consider how we may spur one another on toward love and good deeds. (Hebrews 10:24)

14. a. What do these verses say about the value of friends?

b. We tend to think of peer pressure as a harmful thing. What could be the advantages of peer pressure in the kind of support group Miller describes?

Sometimes we seek the wrong kind of friendships. Ken Abraham asks us to consider the high price of compromising our values in order to gain the acceptance of nonbelieving friends (pages 128-129). He recalls a time when he made a small compromise, trying to please his nonChristian friends, only to find that they were not impressed by his "open-mindedness."

15. a. Have you ever made compromises to prove that you were "just one of the guys"? What were the results? (Did you feel you made the right choice? How do you feel about it as you look back on the situation?)

b. Have you ever refused to compromise, even at the expense of being considered an oddball? Were there any positive long-term results of having held your ground?

c. Abraham observes, "If you have to compromise your values in order to be accepted, you haven't won a

thing, but you've lost a lot" (page 129). What are
some of the things you lose by such compromise?

    d. Is there ever a time in our relationships with nonbe-
       lievers when compromise is the *right* course of action?
       Give an example to support your view.

THE ROAD TEST

1. Have you chosen your six pallbearers yet?! Keep a permanent list of your six closest friends and make regular notes
on how you can be a true friend to each of them.

2. Start an "Iron Man" club with a few other Christian
men, and meet regularly for mutual encouragement.

3. Look around for a man who seems to be totally friend-
less, and begin reaching out to him in small ways.

PERSONAL CHECKLIST

1.

2.

3.

NOTES
1. Quoted in Robert Andrews, *The Concise Columbia Dictionary of
   Quotations* (New York: Columbia University Press, 1987), page 103.
2. "Using Things and Loving People," by Hal David and Archie Jordan,
   CasaDavid Music and Jack and Bill Music, Los Angeles.

The Promises You Make to Worship and Fellowship

W hy do you go to church? To get the kids to Sunday school? To please your wife? To "put on a good front" in your community? Or have you, like the authors of chapter 8, found church to be an exciting place where you can have a significant impact on the lives of others?

After fulfilling all our responsibilities on the job and at home, it can be tempting to take a passive attitude toward the church we attend. In this lesson we consider two of the primary reasons that we as men need to be actively involved in the life of our church. We'll look at our responsibility to worship our heavenly Father and to have meaningful fellowship with His children—our brothers and sisters in Christ.

FELLOWSHIP
The chapter introduction by Gary Smalley and John Trent underscores the tremendous need for each of us to have regular input in the lives of other believers (pages 141-142). Trent tells the touching story of a man who took his two-year-old daughter out for breakfast. As they began to eat, he began telling her how much he appreciated her:

> "Jenny," he said, "I want you to know how much I love you and how special you are to Mom and me. We prayed for you for years, and now that you're here and growing up to be such a wonderful girl, we couldn't be

more proud of you."

Once he said all this, he stopped talking and reached over for his fork to begin eating, but he never got the fork into his mouth.

Jenny reached out and laid her little hand on her father's. His eyes went to hers, and in a soft, pleading voice she said, "Longer, Daddy . . . longer."

He put his fork down and told her even more reasons why he and my daughter-in-law loved her. "You're very kind, nice to your sister, full of energy. . . ." Then, he again reached for his fork only to hear the same words again. A second time . . . and a third . . . and a fourth time . . . and each time he heard the words, "Longer, Daddy, longer." (page 141)

1. a. The daughter in this story had a tremendous need for affirmation from her father. How typical is she of young children?

   b. As we grow into our teens and then our adult years, do you think the need for affirmation increases, decreases, or stays about the same? Explain.

   c. Are there people in your church who seem to be lacking in self-esteem? Could words of affirmation from you be of help to any of them? Who are they?

Paul exhorted us, "Do not let any unwholesome talk come out of your mouths, but only what is helpful for building others up according to their needs, that it may benefit those who listen" (Ephesians 4:29).

2. Have you ever had the experience of "building up" another person? How would you describe this person "before" and "after" you became involved in his or her life?

Jerry White quotes Solomon to stress how much we need each other as Christians (pages 143-145): "Two are better than one because they have a good return for their labor. For if either of them falls, the one will lift up his companion. But woe to the one who falls when there is not another to lift him up" (Ecclesiastes 4:9-10, NASB).

3. a. White says we should *invite* other people to help us when we need help. Do you agree that you should do that? Why, or why not?

   b. What do you think makes that hard for men to do?

White reminds us that we as men need to be accountable to other Christian men. He says we should think especially about being accountable to a trusted friend for our personal Christian life:

We need accountability for our personal lives, our ministries, and our families. Of the three, personal-life accountability is most crucial, since the latter two are more visible. Personal life could include such things as quiet time, prayer, Scripture memory, Bible study, a sin or habit we are trying to conquer, exercise, witness-ing—or any other areas of personal need God brings to mind. (page 144)

4. a. To what extent do you agree? In what areas of your personal life would you be willing to be accountable to a friend?

   b. What risks are involved in making yourself account-able to someone else?

   c. Are the benefits of this kind of accountability worth the risks? Support your answer.

5. Reread Ecclesiastes 4:9-10 (quoted on page 75 of this guide). Have there been times in your life when two have been better than one—that is, when your wife or a friend did something for you that you could never have done for yourself? Talk about that.

In lesson 4 we considered a healthy kind of independence that allows us as men to stand up for what we believe in. White says that Hollywood idealizes an unhealthy kind of independ-ence—an independence that says, "I am totally self-sufficient, and accountable to no one":

The glamorized American West produced the image of the macho man. He is a loner—fiercely independent. He is tough, strong, handsome. The capable, independent woman is his female counterpart. Cigarette and liquor ads paint them indelibly in our minds as accountable to no one—totally self-sufficient. (page 143)

6. a. To what extent do you find yourself wanting to fit that image—wanting to be totally self-sufficient?

   b. What are the benefits of self-sufficiency?

   c. What are the pitfalls (see Hebrews 3:13 on page 70 of this guide, and Hebrews 12:18)?

7. a. How does the Bible's teaching about mutual encouragement differ from the view popular in our self-sufficient society?

   I am the captain of my fate,
   I am the master of my soul.[1]

   b. Should a Christian man ever view himself as a "self-made man"? Explain.

Andrew LePeau talks about the good that can result when we "bring out the best" in others (pages 146-148):

> Praise has mysterious powers. I have watched how the use and abuse of affirmation has tilted the outcome of more than one volleyball game. Those teams that cheer the efforts their members make and don't step in to take away shots from each other find themselves on top of more talented teams who carp, complain, and criticize each other at every flub, flaw, and fault. . . .
>
> People tend to live up to our expectations of them. When we speak positively about them, their own view of themselves is affected. They change and grow under our influence. (pages 147-148)

8. a. How have you been encouraged by the positive comments of others? (By your parents? By a school teacher or athletic coach? By a friend?)

  b. How have you been discouraged by criticism?

  c. Do you know anyone who would value a word of encouragement from you right now? What could you say to that person?

A lot of Christians choose the church they attend mainly on the basis of what that church has to offer them. Many even attend more than one church—one for good teaching; one for exciting worship; one because it has a good Sunday school for the kids,

78

and so on. Luis Palau urges us to think of our local church, not in terms of what we can get, but what we can give:

> One habit we have when getting ready to leave the house on Sunday morning is to take certain expectations about what we want to get out of church and leave them home with the dog. Our goal when we go to church isn't to get, but to give. (page 153)

9. What kinds of things do you look for when choosing which church you will become a part of?

Palau gives some specific suggestions of ways we can give to our church:

> Whatever we do for the least of God's family, we actually do for Him. Don't wait until someone asks you to do something. Volunteer to serve in some capacity. Take the initiative to invite folks—especially singles—to join you for Sunday dinner. Show hospitality to your church's missionaries when they're home on furlough. As a family, visit the sick and the elderly. Take food to those facing financial difficulties. (page 153)

10. a. Which of these "gift ideas" could work for you and your family?

    b. What ideas would you add to that list?

The Bible says that each of us has something to offer our church: "Just as each of us has one body with many members, and these members do not all have the same function, so in Christ we who are many form one body, and each member belongs to all the others" (Romans 12:4-5).

11. Why do you think it is important that each of us contribute his particular gifts and talents to the life of the local church?

WORSHIP
When at church we have many opportunities to affirm and "praise" one another, but the primary reason we are there is to praise God.

12. We read in John 4:23 that God "seeks" our worship. That doesn't mean He *needs* our worship, like people need words of affirmation. If God does not need our worship, why do you suppose He desires it?

13. a. In the First Commandment, God says, "You shall have no other gods before me" (Exodus 20:3). In today's world, what other "gods" can we be tempted to worship?

    b. Which false "gods" have been particular problems in your life?

The following quote is attributed to G. K. Chesterton: "When a man ceases to believe in God, he doesn't believe in nothing; he believes in anything." As the people of the United States move away from their Christian heritage, many tend, as Chesterton suggests, to believe in "anything." Consider the popularity of the New Age movement, which encourages people to paste together their own belief system out of a buffet of sources.

14. How does that tendency to "believe anything" relate to the Bible's emphasis on our need to worship God regularly?

King David was Israel's greatest military leader. He was also a man who enjoyed worshiping God. He wrote, "I love the house where you live, O LORD, the place where your glory dwells" (Psalm 26:8); and "I rejoiced with those who said to me, 'Let us go to the house of the LORD'" (Psalm 122:1).

15. a. Do you "rejoice" at the thought of going to church to worship God? If not, are there any obstacles in you that prevent you from enjoying it? Write down those obstacles. Here are some possibilities to start your thinking:

- Sin you haven't confessed (Psalm 24:3-4)
- Arrogance (Psalm 51:17)
- An offense against someone that you have not dealt with (Matthew 5:23-24)
- Preoccupation with worries, pleasures, or material possessions (Luke 8:14)

b. What can you do to remove these or other obstacles to worship from your life?

From what he shares with us in his psalms, David must have found time for worship even in the midst of battle:

> Though an army besiege me,
>   my heart will not fear;
> though war break out against me,
>   even then will I be confident.
> One thing I ask of the LORD,
>   this will I seek:
> that I may dwell in the house of the LORD
>   all the days of my life,
> to gaze upon the beauty of the LORD
>   and to seek him in his temple.
> For in the day of trouble
>   he will keep me safe in his dwelling.
>   (Psalm 27:3-5)

16. a. Have you found that worship refreshes you, helping prepare you to get back into the battle on Monday morning? If so, how does it do that? If not, why do you suppose it doesn't?

b. What Sunday activities hinder you from benefiting from "the Lord's Day"?

The prophet Isaiah valued time spent in the house of the Lord:

> Many peoples will come and say,
> "Come, let us go up to the mountain of the LORD,
>   to the house of the God of Jacob.
> He will teach us his ways,
>   so that we may walk in his paths." (Isaiah 2:3)

17. Do you often find the worship experience to be a time of learning about God? How could the worship services at your church become more of a learning experience for all involved?

18. a. If a mighty warrior like David can find fulfillment in worshiping God, why is it that, as Robert Hicks points out (pages 154-156), we men often feel "out of place" at church?

    b. Do you agree with Hicks that the church has become too "feminized"? Support you answer.

    c. Hicks talks about an "all male" worship service in the Australian outback. What do *you* think should be done to make the ordinary church service more appealing to men? (Does the change need to come primarily on the part of the church, or on the part of the men who do not enjoy it?)

THE ROAD TEST

1. Choose at least one area of your life in which you would like to see some improvement. Ask your wife or a trusted male friend to check on your progress in that area at a specified future date.

2. As you read your Bible during the week, if you come across a verse you think will encourage someone in your church, jot it down and then give it to that person on Sunday morning.

3. Plan an extended time of worship for one of your church's all-male events. Plan ahead for each participant to have an active role.

PERSONAL CHECKLIST

1.

2.

3.

NOTE

1. William Ernest Henley, quoted in John Bartlett, *Familiar Quotations* (Boston: Little, Brown, 1968), page 815.

The Promises You Make to Your Work

Unless you recently lost a rich uncle, discovered gold, or received a personal phone call from Ed McMahon, you will probably spend a good part of the rest of your life working. Gary Smalley and John Trent set the tone for this chapter by addressing the issue of whether or not we as men have our whole identity wrapped up in what we do for a living:

> Men are most fulfilled in their work when it doesn't
> have to fulfill them. Of the marks of masculinity, self-
> confidence lends the most important help here. When
> we're assured of our worth in God's sight, we don't
> have to let our work define our inner self. This frees
> us to be our best, and not worry about what we do.
> (page 157)

1. a. Whenever two men meet for the first time, one of the first things they find out about each other is what they do for a living. Do you think that most men take their identity from their work?

b. Do you think that most men look to their job for a sense of fulfillment in life? What has been your own experience in this regard?

c. Why do you suppose that has been true for you?

2. a. What attitude should we have about how we earn our living?

   Serve wholeheartedly, as if you were serving the Lord, not men, because you know that the Lord will reward everyone for whatever good he does, whether he is slave or free. (Ephesians 6:7-8)

   b. While there aren't exactly "slaves and masters" in our culture today, there are employees and employers. What do these verses promise to those of us who must be satisfied with "menial" occupations?

   c. How can routine work, such as on an assembly line, be seen as serving the Lord?

Here's what some famous people have said about work:

> I like work; it fascinates me. I can sit and look at it for hours.[1]

> By working faithfully eight hours a day, you may eventually get to be a boss and work twelve hours a day.[2]

> My father taught me to work; he did not teach me to love it.[3]

3. What is the common thread in these men's attitudes about earning their daily bread? How do their attitudes differ from Paul's?

Here's what another famous man said about work:

> When I surveyed all that my hands had done
> and what I had toiled to achieve,
> everything was meaningless, a chasing after the wind.
> (Ecclesiastes 2:11)

Solomon, of all people, should have found fulfillment in his work. Earlier in Ecclesiastes we learn of his many "professional accomplishments" (1:12–2:9).

4. What does his ultimate dissatisfaction say about our efforts to find a fulfilling career?

Solomon did reach a firm conclusion about where fulfillment *could* be found:

> Now all has been heard;
>> here is the conclusion of the whole matter:
> Fear God and keep his commandments,
>> for this is the whole duty of man.
>> (Ecclesiastes 12:13)

Our Lord Jesus, while He walked upon the earth, had a "job." On many occasions He expressed His attitude about His work. For instance, He said, "As long as it is day, we must do the work of him who sent me. Night is coming, when no one can work" (John 9:4).

5. a. What, exactly, was Jesus' work?

   b. What was His attitude toward His work?

   c. In what sense do we as Christian men share in that work?

   d. How does our work for Jesus relate to the work we do for our regular paychecks?

   e. What kind of "hours" do we keep in our work for the Lord?

James Dobson talks about balancing our responsibilities at work with our responsibilities at home (pages 158-162). He asserts,

> In twentieth-century America, it is almost inevitable that a vigorous competition arises between a man's job and his home. Achieving a balance between two areas of responsibility requires constant vigilance, and quite frankly, most men tip the scales dramatically in the direction of their employment. (page 158)

6. a. Has that been your experience? In the battle of priorities, does the "home front" usually lose out to the work place? Why is that the case?

   b. Can you identify with Dobson's story of the effect of overwork on his marriage (pages 159-160)? Cite an example.

Dobson says every man he knows is overcommitted:

> I don't even know any men who aren't running at a breathless pace—my physician, my lawyer, my accountant, my handyman, my mechanic, my pastor, my next-door neighbor. There is symbolic sweat on the brow of virtually every man in North America. (page 161)

The Lord Jesus spoke to people who are running at a breathless pace to earn a living. His advice is found in a passage we looked at in lesson 5:

"So do not worry, saying, 'What shall we eat?' or 'What shall we drink?' or 'What shall we wear?' For the pagans run after all these things, and your heavenly Father knows that you need them. But seek first his kingdom and his righteousness, and all these things will be given to you as well." (Matthew 6:31-33)

7. What answer does Jesus give to our *financial* problems as providers for our families? Explain in your own words.

Dobson questions whether his overcommitted friends truly realize that they're working too much and seeing their families too little:

> Most of these husbands and fathers will admit that they're working too hard, but an interesting response occurs when this subject is raised. They have honestly convinced themselves, and will tell you with a straight face, that their overcommitment is a result of temporary circumstances. A slower day is coming. A light shines at the end of the dark tunnel. (page 161)

8. How is it possible that a Christian man can work himself to death for the sake of his family, while never even spending any time with them? (What is he deceived about?)

In *God in the Dock*, C. S. Lewis wrote about political philosophers who seem to forget about the individual men and women their grandiose "five year plans" are supposed to benefit. The principle applies equally to the overworked dad who forgets the family his job promotion was supposed to benefit:

To the materialist things like nations, classes, civilizations must be more important than individuals, because the individuals live only seventy odd years each and the group may last for centuries. But to the Christian, individuals are more important, for they live eternally, and races, civilizations and the like, are in comparison the creatures of a day.[4]

9. What is your response to that statement? How is it relevant to you?

As we labor at our jobs to provide for our families, we often find ourselves in situations where we have the opportunity to compromise our beliefs as Christian men. The last four authors in this chapter deal with temptations of the work place.

Ken Abraham (pages 163-165) talks about the temptations that especially go with job-related travel:

How sad that adultery has become an "acceptable risk" among business travelers. But sexual immorality, as prevalent as it may be, is only one of the devil's devious devices designed to destroy the frequent traveler. Many others are equally devastating: Self-indulgent vices such as over-eating, "throwing back a few brewskies with the boys," viewing dirty movies "in the privacy of your hotel room," or surrendering to loneliness, self-pity, or laziness. Things you would reject immediately at home somehow seem acceptable on the road. (page 163)

Abraham offers three principles to help us keep our behavior consistent no matter where we are. In the book (pages 164-165) he gives helpful hints for applying each of these principles:

• Keep your spiritual priorities straight.
• Avoid temptation.
• Maintain accountability.

10. When you travel, how can you personally put these principles into practice?

Jay Carty (pages 166-167) and John Brown (pages 168-169) discuss the dangers of making small moral compromises on the job. Carty passes on advice he once received: "Don't take the first $5." Yielding to small temptations, says Carty, nearly always leads to more sins with more far-reaching consequences. Carty and Brown both name actions that they say amount to taking the first $5:

- "Borrowing" from ministry funds
- The first wayward glance
- Lying to avoid trouble
- Secretly using company equipment for personal needs
- Calling in sick when simply wanting time off
- Padding the expense account

Other examples include:

- Allowing a job interviewer to think you're more experienced than you actually are
- Failing to advise a customer about a potential problem with a product
- Grabbing a quick after-lunch nap while the office door is closed

11. From your own observations or personal experience, what would you add to that list?

12. Consider whether you have ever told yourself the two common excuses Brown notes for petty on-the-job pilfering. What is the danger of such rationalization?

- "Everybody does it."
- "It's the least the company can do for me, after all I've done for them."

The word of God is living and active. Sharper than any double-edged sword, it penetrates even to dividing soul and spirit, joints and marrow; it judges the thoughts and attitudes of the heart. Nothing in all creation is hidden from God's sight. Everything is uncovered and laid bare before the eyes of him to whom we must give account. (Hebrews 4:12-13)

He [God] will bring to light what is hidden in darkness and will expose the motives of men's hearts. (1 Corinthians 4:5)

13. How can these biblical principles help keep us "above reproach" in our work place?

14. What decisions do you need to make regarding workplace ethics?

Donald Harvey says that Christians in the work place may sometimes need to put personal relationships ahead of business concerns (pages 170-171). He cites the example of Philemon, whom Paul urged to take back a servant who had deserted him.

15. Have you ever extended grace in a job-related situation where your business instincts told you to do otherwise? Talk about your experience.

THE ROAD TEST

1. Keep a notebook of "spiritual truths I've learned on the job" and pass those insights along to your family or friends.

2. If it is possible in your line of work, arrange for each of your children to spend some time with you on the job.

3. Before your next business trip, plan several edifying activities to occupy your idle time as you travel or stay in your hotel room.

PERSONAL CHECKLIST

1.

2.

3.

NOTES

1. Jerome K. Jerome, quoted in Robert Andrews, *The Concise Columbia Dictionary of Quotations* (New York: Columbia University Press, 1987), page 288.
2. Robert Frost, quoted in Andrews, page 289.
3. Abraham Lincoln, quoted in Andrews, page 288.
4. C. S. Lewis, *God in the Dock* (Grand Rapids, MI: Eerdmans, 1970), page 109.

The Promises You Make to Your Neighbors and Community

Someone has observed that, in many communities in the United States, it is possible for a person to be born into a Christian home, attend Christian schools from kindergarten through college, find a job where he or she is surrounded by Christians, shop at places of business run by Christians, attend Christian music concerts, plan family vacations at Christian retreat centers, and spend his or her retirement days at a Christian retirement center. In short, it is possible for a person to go from cradle to grave having almost no interaction with the world of nonbelievers!

Surely our Lord had something else in mind for us as Christian men. Gary Smalley and John Trent urge us to think of ways to broaden our influence for Christ:

> There is an ever-widening circle of responsibilities
> we have as we seek to be the kind of men God wants
> us to be. In this book we started with God, moved to
> ourselves, then to our wives. With these, our intimacy
> should be the greatest. Then comes family, those with
> whom we worship, and our friends.
>
> Our next circle of interaction is with our fel-
> low workers, our neighbors, community, and nation.
> Remember Jesus' words, "You shall be my witnesses
> in Jerusalem, and in all Judea and Samaria, and to the
> ends of the earth" (Acts 1:8). (page 173)

1. In your own life as a Christian, have you been able to influence an "ever-widening circle" of people? What factors account for that?

Jesus says this about the kind of influence we as Christian men should have in our communities:

> "You are the salt of the earth. . . . You are the light of the world. A city on a hill cannot be hidden. Neither do people light a lamp and put it under a bowl. Instead they put it on its stand, and it gives light to everyone in the house. In the same way, let your light shine before men, that they may see your good deeds and praise your Father in heaven." (Matthew 5:13-16)

2. a. In Bible times, salt was used primarily as a preservative for foods. What do you think it means to be the "salt of the earth"?

   b. Jesus says we should let our lights shine so that unbelievers will see our "good deeds" and be drawn to Him. What sorts of good deeds do you think He's talking about?

3. Choose a nonChristian you have contact with already. How can you become a positive influence on that person for Christ? What is one thing you can do (avoid typical one-time bombardments, such as giving a tract)?

Chuck Miller tells of an opportunity he had to share the gospel with an important public figure, who came to faith in Christ as a result (pages 174-175). He encourages us not to write people off as unreachable, without at least making an effort to tell them about Christ.

4. Why might we assume that certain kinds of people are not interested in the gospel?

Gary Oliver says that we can begin being the "light of the world" only as we get our own moral houses in order—only as we let the light of God's truth shine into every corner of our own hearts (pages 176-179). The two processes must go hand in hand. If we want to help improve the moral tone of our community, we also need to be working on our own commitment to biblical morality.

5. a. What moral problems do you see in your community? Make a list.

b. What hinders you from making a difference in those situations?

c. Choose one of those issues to begin praying about. Oliver outlines five steps you can take to address it (pages 178-179).

Sometimes we are faced with community-wide moral issues such as racism, abortion, or violence in the schools. At other times the issue may involve just one person. Chuck Miller tells about a time when he was asked to help a young man get his life back on track (pages 180-181).

6. As you read Miller's segment, what particular names come to your mind—people whose lives have been "derailed," whom you could help in some way?

Miller was able to guide the young man to a profession of faith in Christ. Involvement in personal evangelism shows that people are more open to the gospel during times of personal crisis.

7. Are you prepared to explain the gospel in simple terms to a person in need? What steps can you take to become better prepared?

THE ROAD TEST

1. Keep a running account of what kind of influence you are having for Christ in each of these areas, as it relates to your own life:

- Jerusalem (family, church, closest friends)
- Judea/Samaria (local community)
- Ends of the earth (ends of the earth!)

2. Get involved in a "social issue" or a rezoning dispute in which you know nonChristians will be involved. Pray that God will give you opportunities for witness as you work with your neighbors toward a common goal.

3. Be alert to "crisis" situations in the lives of nonbelieving friends—deaths in their family, job loss, natural disasters, etc. Pray for sensitivity as to how you can minister and, when possible, present the gospel, during such times.

PERSONAL CHECKLIST

1.

2.

3.

The Promises You Make to Those in Need

Chapter 11 of *What Makes a Man?* focuses on our responsibility as men to those around us who are in need. First we will consider those with physical or material needs, then we will turn our attention to those in spiritual need.

PHYSICAL AND MATERIAL NEEDS

One response to human need was exemplified by the priest and Levite in Jesus' parable of the good Samaritan—seeing the need, and crossing to the other side of the street (Luke 10:30-36). That is also the response of many in more recent times. The atheist philosopher Friedrich Nietzsche once said, "Beggars should be abolished. It annoys one to give to them, and it annoys one not to give to them."[1]

Nietzsche found beggars to be inconvenient. Udo Middelman (pages 196-197) shows us that such inconveniences are a way of life—they were a large part of Jesus' life, and they should be a part of life for those of us who claim to be His disciples:

> It is hard to understand that the Bible calls all of us to be servants. Maybe that is something for nurses, but not for doctors. Secretaries may be expected to work tirelessly. When we think about it, we could include cab drivers, a few full-service gas station attendants, and "lower" jobs that require little mental activity, but full dedication.

Jesus Christ came as a servant. He gave His life for us. He did not have a "normal" life, because He loved us and took on the form of a servant. (page 196)

1. a. Are jobs that "require little mental activity, but full dedication" of any lesser importance than those requiring greater mental skills? Why is it that people tend to look down on such jobs?

   b. When you perform tasks that you perceive as being far below your mental abilities—such as doing routine chores at your church or using your car to run errands for someone—what is your response?

Consider this description of the Lord Jesus:

Your attitude should be the same as that of Christ Jesus: Who, being in very nature God, did not consider equality with God something to be grasped, but made himself nothing, taking the very nature of a servant, being made in human likeness. And being found in appearance as a man, he humbled himself and became obedient to death—even death on a cross! (Philippians 2:5-8)

2. What attitudes did Jesus display that made Him a model of servanthood?

Christ served people constantly. He worked long hours healing sick people in the crowds that pursued Him. He did the job of

102

the lowest household slave when He washed His disciples' feet. But He always served with a purpose.

Middelman notes,

> [Christ] was not mindless, without a concern of his own, without a strategy, a purpose, or a goal. He was not unskilled, or pushed around by the demands of others. He did not just do what others asked Him to do.
>
> His service expressed His will and ability to accomplish what was necessary. He knew exactly what was needed. He knew the problems and the solution. He managed to accomplish his task. He taught us what is true and put our foolishness to shame. He served us well, for without His work there would be no true human life, no hope, no peace, and no new life in righteousness. (pages 196-197)

3. a. What was one of Jesus' goals in washing His disciples' feet (John 13:4-17)?

   b. How did He turn the inconvenient interruption in Bethsaida into an opportunity for ministry (Luke 9:10-17)?

4. How could the notion of being "a servant with a purpose" help you be responsive to opportunities to serve—no matter how menial the service?

Middelman continues the theme of purposeful servanthood, but he takes it one step further. He says that we, as Christian men, should be "interventionists" in our fallen world:

> Religion usually binds people to the way things always are. They submit to the greater circle of life, nature, mud, and normality. The God of the Bible, by contrast, awakens courage. He calls us out of these finite, impersonal and mostly impassionate things.
>
> For the Bible tells us that we live in a world of need. We live after the Fall. Normality, as it is now, is not what God had in mind. Thorns and thistles are to be repelled, floods harnessed, death fought, and justice sought. (pages 200-201)

The Bible teaches that humankind chose to rebel against God, and that this rebellion has brought death and destruction into the world. But God, in the person of Jesus Christ, has brought redemption to all who will accept it.

5. How can each of us, as Christian men, participate with God in "redeeming" our fallen world?

6. According to the following scripture, what job, assigned to man before the Fall, do we still need to perform, as a part of taking care of our fallen world?

> God said, "Let us make man in our image, in our likeness, and let them rule over the fish of the sea and the birds of the air, over the livestock, over all the earth, and over all the creatures that move along the ground." (Genesis 1:26)

7. As caretakers of God's earth, what should be our attitude when there is a seeming conflict between "environmental concerns" and the need for jobs? (Is the answer to that question always clear?)

8. a. As God's representatives on earth, what do you think our attitude toward the homeless should be?

   b. Toward people suffering from AIDS?

   c. Toward anyone who is suffering because of wrong choices he has made?

Middelman sees even the ordinary tasks of everyday life as a part of our exercising dominion over the fallen and often hostile world of nature:

> God thinks it is important to put food on the table. Shelter is urgent in an inhospitable world. The world needs to be measured accurately, so that ships can go and return with cargo. Planes fly only when we dare to be precise, when getting there is important. Paintings should give a true perspective. Marriages are worth a lifetime of investment, struggle, admission, and forgiveness for the sake of a unique relationship.
>
> Against the opposition of nature, we harness water, wind, and fire. Even the light of the sun gets squeezed through a wire into the lights of our homes, factories, and hospitals. We dare to demand a longer

day to work, to read, and to produce than would naturally be ours in winter months.

We dare to tread without fear because we are God's children, not nature's pawns. We are stewards of our high calling as people made in God's image. (page 201)

9. Have you ever felt like "nature's pawn"? What events or circumstances have made you feel that way?

10. How should being made "in God's image" give a sense of importance to even the routine tasks we perform every day?

Anyone who has ever been unemployed knows what it is to feel like nature's pawn! Luis Palau urges us to maintain an attitude of purposeful servanthood even during stressful times such as unemployment (pages 198-199).

Palau offers a four-point plan, which if adhered to, should prevent any of us from feeling out of control. For example, he advises an unemployed person to plan his time carefully, including time for Bible study, job search, and ministry.

11. What are some ways you can use idle time to minister? Palau suggests several things. Can you think of others?

SPIRITUAL NEED
The section in this chapter by Wellington Boone addresses both physical and spiritual needs (pages 184-191). He says that the

church must respond to both physical and spiritual needs, if it is to respond adequately to either. Boone asserts,

> The plight of the inner cities is one of the greatest opportunities God has ever had to manifest His power. Poverty, drugs, out-of-control sex, crime, venereal disease, abortion, murder. The problems cry out for a solution, but for the most part only the humanists have tried to solve them. Unbelievers have put the church to shame, because they have had a zeal to find answers to the problems of the inner cities, while the church has had a zeal mainly for itself. (pages 190-191)

12. a. Do you agree or disagree with Boone's assessment? (Has the church deserted the inner city? Have unbelievers put the church to shame in this regard? How about in the particular area where you live?) Talk about this.

   b. Do you agree that the present crisis in our cities is "one of the greatest opportunities God has ever had to manifest His power"? Explain.

Far from blaming suburban whites for the problems of the black inner city, Boone says that much of the black community's present crisis is due to its own spiritual failings:

> Today, many inner-city blacks have lost the kind of God-centered, generational vision that says life is something worth saving. Fathers are unable to give vision to their children. Black leaders have not given vision to their people.

As a result, the inner city has become dominated by man-centered substitutes like humanism, Islam, and black pride and nationalism. Blacks as an ethnic group do not know where they are going. All they can do is look for answers in the past, especially in blaming the way they were treated by whites. Disengaging themselves from the real problem—their abandonment of Jesus Christ—they look on helplessly as their families and communities disintegrate. (page 185)

13. How much of what Boone says about the black community do you think is true of American society as a whole? Is your own community characterized by an "abandonment" of its religious heritage? If so, what has been the result?

Boone closes on a very positive note: "When the church gets right with God, the lost will see His power and run to Him to be saved" (page 191).

14. a. Do you believe that a revival among the members of your own local church could lead to many men and women finding salvation? Why, or why not?

    b. If you believe that, what steps are you prepared to take to help make it happen in your church?

Luis Palau continues the theme of our need to seek out and help those in spiritual need (pages 194-195). Palau says that, all too often, we assume people are not open to the gospel:

> Some Christians don't say a word to others about Jesus Christ and what He's done for them because they think the lost are happy "just the way they are." They apparently have no concept of what pain, suffering, hurt, guilt, and loneliness many of their work associates, neighbors, and acquaintances are experiencing. (page 194)

Palau goes on to tell about his own failure to share the gospel with his next-door neighbor, who eventually committed suicide.

15. a. What people in your neighborhood might you have an opportunity to speak with about Jesus Christ?

b. Are there people with physical needs whom you could help, thus giving you the opportunity to address their spiritual needs? What is one step you could take?

Some people seem to "have it all together" but may actually be searching desperately for answers to their spiritual questions. Palau observes,

> I have found that some of the people I considered the most closed to the gospel often were the most receptive. Although outwardly they may have feared it, in their hearts they welcomed the message of the good news of Jesus Christ. (page 195)

16. Has the fear of offending your friends prevented you from discussing your faith with them? Why do you think you're afraid?

Jesus said, "No one can come to me unless the Father who sent me draws him, and I will raise him up at the last day" (John 6:44).

17. How should that truth "take the pressure off" as we witness to our unsaved friends and neighbors?

18. If those who respond to the gospel are "drawn" by God, what is our responsibility to witness to them (Matthew 28:18-20, 2 Corinthians 5:19-20)?

In spite of the various ways people responded to the gospel, the apostle Paul could heartily declare, "I am not ashamed of the gospel, because it is the power of God for the salvation of everyone who believes" (Romans 1:16).

19. Do you ever feel shame about the gospel? Why is that?

Steve Diggs tells an amazing story about an encounter with a "born again" cab driver whose actions didn't quite match his profession of faith (pages 192-193). Diggs challenges us to be consistent in our words and deeds:

Don't our actions sometimes deny that we know God? What about the way we talk on the golf course with our unsaved friends? The opportunities we miss to be a witness? Or, the tactics we use to close a sale? (page 193)

20. What actions of yours do other people see that might encourage them to doubt that Christ is who He claims He is?

Diggs says that the stakes are too great for us to be lukewarm in our testimony for Christ:

Jesus wants His people to be "instant in season and out of season." He wants us to be "salt" in a world that is muddled and unseasoned. He wants us to be mature men who lead and do not have to be led. He wants us to stand powerfully for the right. As Christian men who have families, churches, and businesses to lead, we cannot afford the luxury of having to be wet-nursed ourselves. Simply put, Jesus wants us to either get on or get off:

"I know your deeds, that you are neither cold nor hot; I would that you were cold or hot. So because you are luke-warm, and neither hot nor cold, I will spit you out of My mouth." (Revelation 3:15-16, NASB) (page 193)

21. a. In what areas of your life would you describe yourself as lukewarm?

b. What steps do you need to take to become "hot" as you seek to live out your faith and share it with others?

THE ROAD TEST

1. Are the churches in your community divided along racial or ethnic lines? Plan a worship or service activity that could bring two or more of them together.

2. If you are unemployed, look for others in that circumstance, start an "Unemployed Brothers Brigade," and find service projects you can initiate.

3. Who is the "Saul of Tarsus" in your community—the man least likely to succeed at becoming a Christian? Why not take him on as your special project?!

PERSONAL CHECKLIST

1.

2.

3.

NOTE

1. Quoted in Robert Andrews, *The Concise Columbia Dictionary of Quotations* (New York: Columbia University Press, 1987), page 38.

The Promises You Make to the Future

This final lesson, which covers chapters 12 and 13 in the book, sums up all the previous lessons: *To make a promise to anyone, we have to assume that there will be a future in which that promise will be fulfilled.* Whether our immediate future continues in this life or begins our eternal life in heaven, we make our promises knowing that the things we say and do as sons of God will affect the lives of those we love for good or for ill . . . for all eternity.

What kind of promises are you making? Are you willing to live with the results of those promises for all eternity?

As you contemplate your own future, do you ever feel like an animal in a cage? Gary Smalley and John Trent (pages 203-213) tell about an amazing experiment (done before the days of animal rights!). Dogs bound by harnesses were given electric shocks from which they had no way of escape. Later they received electric shocks in a situation where they *could* escape. Yet none of them even attempted to avoid the latter, avoidable shocks. They had become so accustomed to enduring the pain that they made no effort to escape.

The authors use this story to present the concept of "learned helplessness":

Experiencing a major trauma—from losing our spouse, to losing our job, to losing our parents' blessing— affects us deeply. But for some of us, it not only marks our past, it immobilizes us as we face the future.

Instead of actively trying to solve our problems, we can become passive, dependent, and depressed. In short, we learn that in the face of pain, escape is hopeless. And what's more, we internalize three terrible perspectives on our future. (page 209)

The first of these three perspectives is . . .

Our efforts won't match our achievement.
The authors give the example of Mike, who was passed over for promotion despite all his hard work.

1. a. Have you ever felt that life would never reward your efforts? What setbacks or disappointments or betrayals led to that feeling?

    b. Do the following Bible verses encourage you? Why, or why not?

    God is not unjust; he will not forget your work and the love you have shown him as you have helped his people and continue to help them. (Hebrews 6:10)

    Let us not become weary in doing good, for at the proper time we will reap a harvest if we do not give up. (Galatians 6:9)

The second cause of learned helplessness is the feeling that . . .

The key to happiness is out of reach.

> The man lost on the road to learned helplessness often feels that not only does fate rule us, but it's a cruel fate that puts the single key we need to be happy just out of reach.
>
> Take Brian, for example. He was the older brother. If Dad should have bonded with anyone, it should have been him! Not his younger brother. He wore his heart out to please his father. But no matter how far he stretched toward him, it seemed he could never reach the arms of acceptance he wanted so much.
>
> In a climate of unfair comparison and favoritism, Brian made a subtle, but terribly damaging decision. Deep inside, he equated what he was missing with what he could never become . . . younger. And because he focused on something that could never happen as his key to happiness in the future, it pushed him to committed pessimism . . . and eventually right into clinical depression. (pages 211-212)

2. Are you being kept from a happy future by dwelling on the lack of something you will never have? What is it?

The authors observe that pessimists tend to look to the past while optimists tend to look to the future—often actually wishing they were older! They allude to the words of the apostle Paul (which suggest that he was an optimist):

> One thing I do: Forgetting what is behind and straining toward what is ahead, I press on toward the goal to win the prize for which God has called me heavenward in Christ Jesus. (Philippians 3:13-14)

3. Should our faith in Jesus Christ give us adequate reason to be optimists, despite any negative experiences we have had? Explain you answer.

Third, helpless people often begin to feel that . . .

I'm all alone in my pain.

> During the experiments that first showed learned helplessness, the dogs who had experienced the repeated shocks were verbally, even physically, encouraged to jump the barrier, but they didn't. While the shock was going on, it was like the dogs drew so far into an inner, protective shell that they were oblivious to outside encouragement. (page 212)

4. How can learned helplessness prevent a person from seeking help?

The authors give a warning to those who feel all alone:

> If our efforts don't count, and the key to change is out of reach, then a deep sense of impenetrable loneliness sets in. And if we continue to stumble down the road of inner loneliness, we're on our way to disaster. Whether we realize it or not, we share this road with compulsive gamblers, sexaholics, alcoholics, and child abusers who all have something in common: unending loneliness! (page 213)

The Bible records an unforgettable example of a man who thought he was all alone in his pain. The Old Testament prophet

Elijah was convinced that he was the only faithful prophet left in Israel. And he was weary of the burden of being God's only spokesperson. God found Elijah sleeping in a cave and asked, "What are you doing here, Elijah?"

Elijah replied, "I have been very zealous for the LORD God Almighty. The Israelites have rejected your covenant, broken down your altars, and put your prophets to death with the sword. I am the only one left, and now they are trying to kill me too."

Yet God had a surprising response for this lonely prophet: "Yet I reserve seven thousand in Israel—all whose knees have not bowed down to Baal and whose mouths have not kissed him." (See 1 Kings 19:9-10,18.)

5. a. Have you ever felt, as Elijah did, that you were all alone in your suffering or in your faithfulness to the Lord? Explain.

   b. Why do you suppose Elijah was unaware of the many (seven thousand!) in Israel who were actually on his side?

Having described the wrong way to face the future—learned helplessness—Gary Smalley and John Trent describe the *right* way to face it: learned *hopefulness* (pages 225-232).

6. a. Read Smalley and Trent's counsel for moving from helplessness to hope. Write down three specific ways their counsel is relevant to you.

117

b. What steps can you personally take to pursue hope?

Dennis Rainey talks about a challenge most of us face: the challenge of preparing our children for their future (pages 214-215). He tells of wrestling with selfishness as he drove home from work one evening—wanting time to himself but also wanting to be a good father:

> It's just one night. One night. What will I accomplish? Will I waste it spending all evening in front of the television? Or invest it in planting the seeds of a positive legacy for my children? (pages 214-215)

7. Rainey goes on to tell about what he did with his children that evening. What activities have you done, or can you do, with your children to help give them a solid foundation for the future?

Udo Middelman talks about the need to make our children aware of their history (pages 217-219). He laments the fact that such things as divorce and frequent moves tend to make us lose track of our personal history.

8. Do you see family history as something important for your children to know? What kind of activities could help them learn about their past?

Middelman's main concern is that our children know the history of God's dealings with humankind:

Behind this is the God of the Bible, who alone affirms His image in each person. He, not chance or the unknown, no impersonal primal soup, gives us a name: man. He tells us of the Fall in history, when things fell apart to leave us broken, fragile, and outside of His garden. The Bible tells us about God's love for His creatures, His running after them to repurchase them in history. Only this way, and in contrast to ancient and modern myths around the world, are we at home, not orphans lost in the cosmos. Without it we are strangers in a world of wild things. (pages 218-219)

9. In a world where so many ideas compete for our allegiance, why is the kind of "history lesson" Middelman speaks of so important?

10. Second Timothy 3:16-17 says the Bible equips a person for life. What is one area in which you would like your children to be equipped that just going to school—even a Christian school—can't teach them?

Bill Hybels says that each one of us can, and should, be a visionary (page 216). The alternative is to simply "go with the flow," and become victims of our circumstances.

11. What visions do you have for your family, your church, or your place of employment? Hybels suggests three ways to categorize those visions. See how many visions you can list under each category.

a. New ways to do something:

b. New ways to improve something:

c. New ways to fix something:

12. What is the one condition God places on our plans, or visions, before promising to help us fulfill them (Proverbs 19:21)?

As our study draws to a close, Fran Sciacca urges us to get "back to the real future": "The real future for the child of God is the life that begins when this one ends" (page 222). He challenges us to reexamine our priorities: Are we truly living for heaven, or are our hopes all set on *this* life?

> To prepare our children, we men must teach them to live now in light of eternity. But we may first have to change how we see ourselves in relation to God and the world around us. This may necessitate serious spiritual heart surgery for us fathers. We need to look deep inside and find out what our own hearts beat for— because our children already know, even if we don't. (page 222)

13. Sciacca says that "our children already know" the answer. Do you agree or disagree? What do your children think of your spiritual commitment?

The Bible describes Christians as "aliens" while they live on this earth:

> They admitted that they were aliens and strangers on earth. (Hebrews 11:13)

> Dear friends, I urge you, as aliens and strangers in the world. (1 Peter 2:11)

> Our citizenship is in heaven. And we eagerly await a Savior from there, the Lord Jesus Christ. (Philippians 3:20)

121

14. a. How do you think we should express our "heavenly citizenship" as we live on this earth?

    b. What should we be doing to help our children claim heaven as their true homeland?

    c. What should be our attitude toward the "citizens of this world"?

Sciacca says that some of us who should be living like aliens are actually behaving like "tourists":

> Tourists are aliens without allegiance. They look for pleasure, not purpose. Tourists love the world, but are indifferent to the people of it. And, tragically, tourists are often offensive and rude to the real residents. (page 223)

15. What signs of being a tourist have been evident in your behavior recently?

Finally, this challenge: "There will come a day at a point in history when we will exit this life and become permanent residents in the presence of God. Do you live in light of that fact?" (page 223).

The closing remarks by Bill McCartney underscore the serious choices all people must make about this life and about where we will spend eternity (pages 233-234). McCartney reminds us that there are really only two choices, in Jesus' words:

"Enter through the narrow gate. For wide is the gate
and broad is the road that leads to destruction, and
many enter through it. But small is the gate and narrow
the road that leads to life, and only a few find it."
(Matthew 7:13-14)

16. a. How can we be sure that we are among the "few" who have found the road that leads to eternal life?

    b. How can we help assure that our children have found or will find that road, and will therefore have a "real future"?

THE ROAD TEST

1. It has been shown that the moments right after a satisfying meal are the best time to influence a person for good or ill. Plan a series of "after dinner enrichment times" for your

family. These include reading Scripture, as well as things like reading and discussing stories from the daily newspaper.

2. Ask your pastor or another knowledgeable person for suggestions on books or videos presenting a "biblical world view" on issues your children are studying in school.

3. Plan trips to the birthplaces of as many family members as time and distance allow.

PERSONAL CHECKLIST
1.

2.

3.

Note to Leaders

The number of lessons in this book is designed so that it can be used in a regular Sunday school quarter or other small groups. This material could also benefit two people going over it together or an individual working through it alone.

But studying these lessons with a group can help accomplish several things: (1) A group may help some people realize that others are suffering in the same way they are. (2) Group members encourage one another. (3) Groups can also help to keep us from misinterpretation.

When leading a group, always start on time and begin with prayer. The Holy Spirit gives us understanding, so ask Him for that at the outset. Ask the others to bring their Bibles, pen, and paper. Writing things down is not only therapeutic, but it also helps memory retention.

Try to involve everyone. Be sensitive, and pray for discernment. Your ability to draw people into the discussion may be the most important thing you can accomplish.

Keep the conversation relaxed. Emphasize that no question is bad or not worth asking. Listen carefully, be affirming, and take every question seriously.

If you don't know an answer, admit it. Encourage the group to consider and pray about the question during the next week.

Above all, attempt to be a source of encouragement to one another.

About Promise Keepers

Promise Keepers is an organization dedicated to motivating men toward greater strength and Christlike masculinity.

Promise Keepers sponsors men's conferences in regional locations and various churches around the country. The annual Promise Keepers National Men's Conference is held each July in Boulder, Colorado.

Promise Keepers seeks to be a supply line to the local church, helping to encourage and assist pastors and ministry leaders in calling men to an accountable relationship with Jesus Christ and with one another. Promise Keepers wants to provide men's materials (like this guide) as well as seminars and the annual conference to emphasize the godly conviction, integrity, and action each of us needs.

Please join us in helping one another be the kind of men God wants us to be. Write or call our offices today.

TO GET INFORMATION
ON OTHER GREAT TOOLS
CALL OR WRITE:
PROMISE KEEPERS
PO Box 103001
Denver, CO 80250-3001
1 (800) 456–7594